the FATHER of all DAD GUIDES

the
FATHER
of all
DAD GUIDES
from (A)DORING to (Z)ADDY

MADELEINE DAVIES + TARA JACOBY

ST. MARTIN'S GRIFFIN · NEW YORK

www.stmartins.com

The Library of Congress Cataloging-in-Publication Data is available upon request.

ISBN 978-1-250-19206-6 (hardcover)
ISBN 978-1-250-19207-3 (ebook)

Our books may be purchased in bulk for promotional, educational, or business use. Please contact your local bookseller or the Macmillan Corporate and Premium Sales Department at 1-800-221-7945, extension 5442, or by email at MacmillanSpecialMarkets@macmillan.com.

First Edition: June 2019

10 9 8 7 6 5 4 3 2 1

To our dads: Bruce, Robin, and Kevin.
Thanks for putting up with us.

CONTENTS

ACKNOWLEDGMENTS

First and foremost, thank you to Jennifer Herrera at David Black Agency. Without her spark of an idea and guidance, this book never would have happened. So much gratitude also goes to Laura Apperson at St. Martin's Press. Not only did she believe in our book, she also held our hands through the publication process and somehow didn't murder us as we missed a deadline or two. Thank you to Jonathan Bennett and the St. Martin's design team for the many back-and-forths and their hard work. Thank you to Gawker Media and Jezebel for being the first to let us work together, blending our art and writing on many crazy projects. And finally, thank you to our friends and loved ones for their support and enthusiasm. We love you so much.

INTRODUCTION

Of all the mammalian species of North America, few are as paradoxically mysterious and demanding of attention as the human father of the United States. Often quiet in his affection and deafeningly loud in his anger, the American dad—as much as we love him—is a particularly exciting study, which is why we've created this guide as an aid for readers to identify themselves (if you happen to be a dad), their dads (if you happen to have a dad), dads on television (often a stand-in when your dad's not around), and dads in the wild.

In *The Father of All Dad Guides: from A(doring) to Z(addy)*, you will learn how to identify fathers through:

- **THEIR MARKINGS:** Some dads have mustaches. Others do not!

- **DAD CALLS:** These include: "I'll turn this car around right now" and "Can't you ask your mom about that?"

- **MIGRATION PATTERNS:** Why does Dad constantly ignore directions when he clearly doesn't know where he is going?

- **HIBERNATION:** Dads are tired all the time.

- **DEFINING CHARACTERISTICS:** All dads are different, but they typically fall into at least one of the categories we've collected here. Is your dad obsessed with barbecuing? He might be a Grill Dad. Did he only really begin to see women as people deserving of political and social equality after he had daughters? That right there is the Feminist Dad! Does he collect guns and canned food in an underground bunker? Yep, your dad's a Prepper! Don't know what a "zaddy" is? It's the word millennials and Gen Zers are using instead of "sugar daddy!" What a world!

But before you start heading down the winding and exciting road that is the study and understanding of American dads, you'll want to ask yourself a few questions:

AM I A DAD?

We don't know! Are you a male identifying person who has, had, or is devoted to the lifelong care of a human child? If the answer is yes, then...yes, you're a dad. Please check in with your kids.

DO I HAVE A DAD?

Probably! Pretty much everyone has a "father," i.e. a man whose sperm fertilized an egg (typically found inside your "mother"), starting the process that would eventually develop into the human being that is you.

That said, not everyone has a "dad" because the word "dad" suggests an active involvement in a child's life that some are unwilling or incapable of providing. This especially awful breed are called "deadbeats" or "absentee fathers," and if you see one, proceed with the utmost caution.

Some people, it's worth noting, have more than one dad! This happens when a dad marries another dad or when your mom, expressing her own mating and migration patterns, marries a lot of men and asks you to call them "dad." You might do it to make her happy, but you'll likely never feel good about it.

DO I HAVE A *NICE* DAD?

There is an approximately 85 percent chance that you have a nice dad, but as you'll learn in the following pages, a decent portion of dads are weirdos and some, we're sorry to tell you, are jerks. Whatever kind of dad you have, you're not alone!

THAT STATISTIC DOESN'T SEEM RIGHT...

It probably isn't. Our dads didn't take the time to tutor us in math.

MY DAD IS NORMAL. IS THIS BOOK STILL FOR ME?

Yes. This book is for everyone with—or without—a dad.

ADORING DAD

The Adoring Dad knows that his child—no matter how much trouble they get in—can do no wrong. (If—and it's very likely—the Adoring Dad's offspring are the worst-behaved kids on the block, you certainly won't hear that from him.) You can identify him by his car (decorated with a "My Child Is on the Honor Roll" bumper sticker) and his living space, which will always include an immaculately preserved version of his child's bedroom that will remain an untouched shrine with trophies and plaques celebrating past accomplishments that even his kid (now an adult) doesn't really care about anymore. But what does that matter! His child won a forensics/football/academic bowl/dance award in 2003 and he won't let any of you forget it.

Keep in mind that pursuing and coupling with the Adoring Dad's child is not recommended because—in the Adoring Dad's eyes, at least—you will never be good enough for their child. If you court them regardless, be prepared for a life of receiving sidelong glances and curt responses from the Adoring Dad. If your relationship ends in divorce, well . . . watch your back.

DO YOU HAVE A JOB?

A. Yes, and I am very happy in it.

B. Yes, and I do not feel professionally satisfied.

C. No, but I am looking for one.

D. No. I'm fine being unemployed.

YOU'RE PICKING MY PROGENY UP FOR A DATE. DO YOU:

A. Come to their door and knock?

B. Text or honk your horn and wait outside?

C. Meet them at the location of the date—it's easier that way?

D. Not take them on a date at all unless they're paying?

HOW MANY CHILDREN DO YOU WANT?

A. However many we can responsibly financially support.

B. 1–2.

C. I do not want to have children.

D. Doesn't matter because I am not supporting them.

IN YOUR MIND, ARE YOU AND MY CHILD "WELL MATCHED"?

A. Yes! We're a perfect team.

B. We're always going to have our differences and that's okay!

C. They're too good for me.

D. I'm too good for them.

BREWMASTER DAD

You don't like bitter or hoppy ales? Well, that's only because you haven't tried the Brewmaster Dad's bitter or hoppy ales! Same goes for stouts, lagers, ambers, IPAs, or any other beer the Brewmaster Dad has produced or is producing in the garage or basement where he's built his makeshift (albeit quite impressive) brewery.

When the Brewmaster Dad lets you try his beer, you must nod and say, "*Mmm,*" no matter what you actually think of the taste. When he tells you the history of IPAs, you'll tell him that you're interested even if you're not. Why? Because the Brewmaster Dad's lectures also come with the promise of, at the very least, a light buzz. He's laid back and affable about everything—duh, the kind of guy you can kick back and have a beer with!—EXCEPT his craft brews. Beer is not a laughing matter.

Unless of course you're talking about light lagers (he hopes you're not), in which case—he'll tell you with a smirk—they're ALL jokes and are not allowed in his home.

a BEER FLIGHT of DADS

LAGER This dad is simple and reliable, so much so that even when he's being a bad dad—flat, lukewarm—he's still kind of good or, at his most terrible, inoffensive. However, he is best in the summer when the grill is going (see Grill Dad on page 40 for more) and when he's chilled out.

WHEAT Light and sweet, this dad can be a little saccharine for some, but others like him with a slice of citrus.

INDIA PALE ALE

An IPA Dad has a little bit of an edge and occasionally he can get a little bitter. He is the dad that all of your friends will think is cool because of his worldly dankness.

STOUT

Not for everyone, this dad has a dark sense of humor despite his frothy top layer. But the people who love him really love him.

COACH DAD

Sure, the Coach Dad might be hard on you, but that's because he sees your full potential and knows you've yet to realize it. Through hard work and tough love, he will teach you what it means to have grit and—more importantly—help you grow into a capable adult who possesses ample integrity and a good work ethic. (Either that or he'll just scream at you at your Little League games. But back to the nice Coach Dad!)

The Coach Dad is typically identified by his khaki shorts, tucked-in, brightly colored polo shirt, team hat, and the whistle around his neck. He is usually found in high school gyms, locker rooms, and football fields around the country. Because he must go where the job goes, his migration patterns are untrackable.

Caution: An encounter with a Coach Dad, especially one held during practice in the pouring rain, can end with a pep talk or an inspirational *Friday Night Lights*-esque speech. Steer clear if you're not ready to believe in yourself.

Clear eyes, full hearts, can't lose.

DAD LIBS!
An Inspiring Halftime Speech

_____
[A type of animal, plural]

It's been an _____ season. We have _____ and we have
[adjective]   [verb, past tense]

_____ and we have _____. Every single one of you
[verb, past tense]   [verb, past tense]

has _____ to get here. And are we going to let our rivals,
[verb, past tense]

the _____s take this _____ away from us? After _____?
[noun]   [noun]   [noun, an event]

I don't think so.

We are down _____ points. Our chances are _____. But
[number]   [adjective]

I know that if we go out there and give it our all, we will come

out ahead. Think of your _____ in the stands. Think of the
[noun]

_____ you want to ask to prom. Think of how good you'll
[noun]

feel when you _____ and take away the _____ cup.
[verb]   [noun]

Most importantly, think of your fellow _____s—they are your
[noun]

teammates and we will do this for each other.

Now when we _____ back out there, we will reenter
[verb]

the _____ as champions, our _____s held high. This is
[place]   [body part]

teamwork and with it no one, not even _____ can stop us.
[noun]

On _____, go _____s!
[number]   [animal]

DOG DAD

The Dog Dad is one of few dads in this book that doesn't require human children to claim fatherhood. Why? Because his pride and joy are not his offspring, but his *canine* children, i.e., his "fur babies." Safe havens for his most vulnerable emotions, dogs provide their Dog Dad with everything that real kids do not: unconditional love, nonjudgmental companionship, and an inability to be disappointed in the Dog Dad's failures.

Whereas many (though not *all* Dog Dads) might be too confined by cultural norms to coo and preen over a child, they will likely have no problem fussing over their pups, maybe even grooming them and enrolling them in pageants (a.k.a. dog shows.) But not every Dog Dad is that fancy: Lots of them adopt pooches from shelters and spend their time at dog parks, lovingly combing ticks out of their dogs' fur and giving them heartworm medication. Whether they'd do this for a person depends on the man, but regardless, DOG will always be the Dog Dad's copilot.

match the
DOG
to the
DAD

EMBARRASSING DAD

No matter what this father intends, the Embarrassing Dad can never *not* embarrass their children. A limit to the ways they can do this has yet to be reached by science, sociologists, or mortified kids, but the most recognizable methods we've observed are:

- Telling bad jokes.
- Bad wedding dancing.
- Not tipping at restaurants.
- Loudly asking your friends or romantic partner humiliating questions with regard to their relationship to you.
- Loudly expressing outdated and often politically incorrect politics.
- Taking holidays too seriously.
- Never knocking before entering your bedroom.

If you recognize this variation of dad in your own parent, the best-case scenario is that his embarrassing nature becomes charming with time. If you recognize this variation of dad because you're an Embarrassing Dad yourself, we're glad you're having fun!

the MOST EMBARRASSING

JACOB
(1750 B.C., Canaan)

In Genesis, Jacob is such an annoying dad to 11 of his 12 sons that they sold Joseph, his favorite, to a group of roaming Ishmaelites, all so they could get their pops to stop doting on Joseph and give them some attention, too. A good lesson in not playing favorites!

KING TUT
(Egypt, 1332 B.C.)

Neither of the pharaoh Tutankhamun's children survived birth, but what qualifies him as an embarrassing dad is that his wife and would-be mother of his children, Ankhesenamun, was also his half-sister AND cousin. And your family feels complicated...

GENGHIS KAHN
(1152 A.D., Mongolia)

Genghis was a rolling stone, to say the least. Legend has it that he had so many children that one out of 200 people living today are in his bloodline. Sadly, he was also a deadbeat who never knew the vast majority of his kids.

POPE ALEXANDER VI
(1474 A.D., Italy)

Pope Alexander VI— also known as Rodrigo Borgia—was the Pope, yes, but he also (against all the rules) fathered at least four children out of wedlock. Explain that to your teacher on career day!

*Dates signify the approximate year when these historic figures became fathers.

DADS in HISTORY

HENRY VIII
(1516 A.D., England)

You think your dad is embarrassing, but imagine if he annulled his marriage to your mom and put her in exile so that he could marry a 25-year-old who he then had beheaded on charges of treason, adultery, and incest. (And she was only the first!) YIKES!!

LEOPOLD MOZART
(1756 A.D., Austria)

Father to Wolfgang Amadeus Mozart, arguably one of the most accomplished and talented composers of all time, ol' Leopold gave up his own music career to focus on his prodigal son, therefore becoming one of history's most prolific stage dads.

JOSEPH SMITH
(1832, United States)

Founding the Church of Latter Day Saints aside, Smith's family life was complicated with his wife—Emma Hale—refusing to recognize her husband's rampant polygamy up until her death. Dinner with your dad's new wife is rough enough, but imagine if he was ALSO still married to your mom.

MICHAEL LOHAN
(1986, United States)

Father to actor Lindsay Lohan, Michael is a known-embarrassment —an unrelenting stage dad who pushed his children's careers to further his own fame. He's been arrested several times, but his worst crime is his infamously bad parenting, which allegedly included selling personal information about his family to the tabloids. Henry VIII is not sounding so bad, huh?

FEMINIST DAD

Congrats to the Feminist Dad, who embraces that women are people and deserving of respect and equality by teaching his children—regardless of their gender—that the sociopolitical struggles of women should be the sociopolitical struggles of *everyone*.

Sure, there's a chance he only realized all this after having a daughter, something you'll be able to notice because he'll not-so-subtly drop hints like "As a father of a daughter, I . . ." when discussing women's issues—but at least he's getting there.

Of course, there are the special few Feminist Dads who have long been feminists, even if they only have sons! To these dads: Good job! We appreciate you even if we gently mock you for still rocking that "I'm with Her" shirt.

A FEMINIST CHECKLIST for NEW DADS of DAUGHTERS

☐ Gender-neutral color scheme (try yellow!) for clothes and room decor.

☐ Actually, strike *that*. Girls can wear blue and boys can wear pink because gender is a social construct!

☐ Actually, strike *that*. Girls can wear pink because there's nothing demeaning about overt displays of femininity.

- [ ] Also it's infantilizing to call her a "girl," even if she is a literal infant. Call her "Womyn-to-Be."

- [ ] Then again, she might not grow up to identify as a woman, so don't put that label on her, either. Just call her by her name!

- [ ] Speaking of names, may we recommend something gender-neutral, like Sydney, Alex, or Glorp?

- [ ] Then again, why do names have genders to begin with? Call her what you want.

- [ ] By which we mean "call her what *she* wants" because it's very important to instill agency in your daughter so she'll grow to understand the power of choice.

- [ ] Instead of the usual bedside stories, mix things up with some light feminist theory, like that of Germaine Greer.

Continues...

- [ ] Reminder, though, that like a lot of second-wave feminists, she's a gender essentialist, so you should probably mix in some modern theory, as well.

- [ ] Another reminder, though: Feminism, like a lot sociopolitical identities, is dominated by white cis voices. Just a little something to keep in mind.

- [ ] One more small thing to keep in mind: The world is notoriously terrible to women and no matter what you do, your daughter will come to understand this through the lack of choices, stereotyping, and representation she encounters legally, institutionally, and socially. Probably even with in her own family because none of us—not even you!—can escape the patriarchy.

- [ ] Have a panic attack.

- [ ] Rent a cabin in the middle of nowhere. Go out in the middle of the night and scream your fears for your daughter at the moon until your voice is gone and you collapse on the ground.

- [ ] Wake up in the woods. Notice the strange markings you've made on your own body with mud while blacked out.

- [ ] Find out that these markings are not random, but primitive symbols of witchcraft. Copy them carefully on a scrap of notebook paper.

- [ ] On the first full moon after your daughter is born, re-create the symbols around her. Burn the notebook page and bury the ashes with a chicken bone and an old copy of *Ms.* magazine in the backyard.

CONGRATS! YOU'RE ON YOUR WAY to BECOMING a FEMINIST DAD

GRILL DAD

D id you touch the grill? We hope not because, as any Grill Dad will tell you, grilling is an art that only a Grill Dad can perfect. The Grill Dad is a seasonal father who hibernates for most the winter, only occasionally climbing out of his cave to tailgate before cold weather sporting events. He is most active in the summer, typically stirring when the weather is above 70 degrees. You can track the Grill Dad by following the scent of cooking meat, the smoke that wafts from his backyard (or on sidewalks in areas where backyards don't exist), or his loud proclamation that while gas grills are easier to use than charcoal grills, nothing beats that charcoal flavor.

While he doesn't really know how to cook anything that can't be put on the grill, the Grill Dad is certain that he is the best chef in the neighborhood, if not the world.

Bon appétit!

HIPPIE DAD

Typically inhabiting left-leaning towns and cities across the country (like Austin, Texas; Portland, Oregon; or Asheville, North Carolina), the Hippie Dad is an idealist, often devoted to causes such as environmentalism, socialism, and—very adamantly—the legalization of marijuana.

With increased age and a growing bank account, the Hippie Dad will often become what's known as a "yippie," a portmanteau of "yuppie" and "hippie." A yippie is a hippie who has softened on his far-left politics and settled comfortably into the upper middle class. Though he will still probably smoke a lot of weed, delve deep into the practice of yoga, and (in his worst form) write endless letters of complaint to local newspapers and businesses, he is a true member of the bourgeoisie, though he'll never admit it. He buys organic and drives a hybrid, after all.

Spot this exciting dad at your local farmers market today!

LIT YOGA POSES *for the* STONER DAD

DEADHEAD STAND

WOODSTOCK WARRIOR 1

WOODSTOCK WARRIOR 2

TAKE IT EASY POSE

DOWNWARD FACING DAD

INVISIBLE DAD

The Invisible Dad is unseen for a multitude of reasons. Maybe he disappeared for good when you discovered his secret family in Tulsa or maybe he still shows up occasionally via a postcard or, if he's truly dedicated to *appearing* dedicated, a visit to take you bowling every month or so.

Also known as the "every other weekend and holidays" dad, the Invisible father can be charming in small doses. You might even know him as the "fun" parent, but that's only because he comes along so rarely that, unlike your mother, he doesn't have to care about whether or not you adhere to "rules" or basic nutrition.

The Invisible Dad does not have one tried-and-true habitat, unless you count "not here" as a particular location. That said, he usually dens in a one-bedroom apartment (maybe with a foldout couch for you and your siblings) that he shares with a line of short-term girlfriends, all probably named Shelly or Debbie.

CREATE

the

DAD YOU NEVER HAD....

(USING THIS EMPTY OUTLINE) —————————————

(OR USE THE SPACE TO SCRIBBLE OUT YOUR ANGER AND DISAPPOINTMENT!)

JOKESTER DAD

Jokester Dad resembles the Embarrassing Dad (sometimes they even overlap), but unlike the Embarrassing Dad, he's either *actually* funny or—at the very least—cute about *not* being funny. This is the dad whose way of showing love and affection is through gentle ribbing and teasing that sometimes, according to the mother of his kid(s), "goes too far." He is the favorite dad of all of his child's friends, which is great because he loves a house full of company, so long as they'll watch Monty Python with him.

To impress a Jokester Dad, come prepared with some old *Mad* magazines or a nonfictional history of *Saturday Night Live*. Want to impress him further? Watch a Richard Pryor documentary or wax poetic about the life and times of Gilda Radner. Or if that feels too daunting, sit back and enjoy what the Jokester Dad has to offer *you*. Entertaining is this dad's favorite activity.

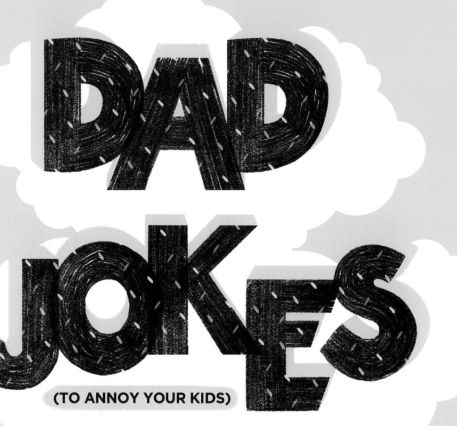

DAD JOKES

(TO ANNOY YOUR KIDS)

- Does your face hurt? **BECAUSE IT'S KILLING ME!**

- Don't play tricks, **THAT'S HOW HOUDINI DIED!**

- I'd rather have a bottle in front of me **THAN A FRONTAL LOBOTOMY.**

- A three legged dog walks into a saloon and says, **"I'M LOOKING FOR THE MAN WHO SHOT MY PAW."**

- A man walked into a bar and said, **"OW."**

- Did you get a haircut? **NO, I GOT THEM ALL CUT.**

- The rotation of Earth **REALLY MAKES MY DAY!**

- Want to hear a joke about a piece of paper? **NEVER MIND, IT'S TEARABLE!**

- To a server at a restaurant after he's cleared his plate: **I HATED IT!**

- To a cashier who asks if he wants his milk in a bag: **NO, I'LL KEEP IT IN THE CARTON!**

- To anyone willing: **PULL MY FINGER.**

KILLJOY DAD

The Killjoy Dad comes in several variations, the two most common being the Overprotective Killjoy and the Current Events Killjoy.

The Overprotective Killjoy sees dangers everywhere: on trampolines (rightfully), carnival rides (also rightfully), recreational sports (Is it just us or does the Overprotective Killjoy have a point?), and in the eyes of strangers. Never will their child be allowed to do what the other kids are doing, even if the other kids' parents say it's okay. Would you jump off a cliff just because Chad or Becky's parents said they could do it? Even if you would, the Overprotective Killjoy wouldn't let you.

The Current Events Killjoy focuses less on seeing the world's endless hazards, instead choosing to view the planet as a ticking time bomb on which we are all doomed. Genocide abroad? He'll tell you all about it when you dare to complain about the cereal choices at breakfast. Fail to clean your room? There are kids in refugee camps who would do anything for their own bedroom, you brat! And don't even get him started on drones, Congress, the internet, organic produce, nonorganic produce, fossil fuels, the electoral college, rising water levels, melting ice caps, Marxism, capitalism, communism, feudalism, any kind of –ism, or modern pop music.

The Current Events Killjoy Dad is often right, but, man, is he a bummer to be around.

ARE YOU ABOUT to LOSE an EYE?

WHAT ARE YOU DOING?

PLAYING OUTSIDE

DO YOU HAVE SUPERVISION?
- YES
- NO

IS IT YOUR DAD?
- YES
- NO

WATCHING TV OR READING A BOOK

ABOUT WHAT?

ROMANCE + FRIENDSHIP

IS IT GIVING YOU CRAZY IDEAS?
- YES
- NO

ACTION + ADVENTURE

IT'S A SAFETY MANUAL

WILL YOU CHECK WITH YOUR DAD AFTER YOU'RE DONE WUTH ANY QUESTIONS YOU MAY HAVE?
- YES
- NO

NOTHING

SEEMS UNLIKELY

YOU ARE PLANNING SOMETHING

ARE YOU PAYING ATTENTION AND TREATING EVERYTHING HE SAYS WITH THE UTMOST SERIOUSNESS AND RESPECT?
YES
NO
YOU WILL LOSE an EYE!
DAD DOESN'T BELIEVE YOU.

LEATHER DADDY

How do we put this delicately? The Leather Daddy is not a dad per se, although he does take obedience and discipline very seriously. He adores leather goods like harnesses, vests, and chaps, though he will occasionally settle for materials closer to latex. He might resemble an animal—say a bear or an otter—and though you can find the Leather Daddy anywhere (check out local bars with names like "The Cock"), he's most open and happy in progressive environments, such as Berlin, New York, or San Francisco.

Still confused? Get out in the world! Visit the Castro on vacation or go to a gay pride march. You'll have fun! We promise!

UNEXPECTED SAFE WORDS

for DADS and LEATHER DADDIES

 A safe word is something you say to let your partner know that you are no longer having a good time. They're as good in sexual fetish communities as they are in your own personal relationships because while it's good to test boundaries, it's even better to communicate and form a safe relationship with your partner. Here are some fun suggestions...for dads!

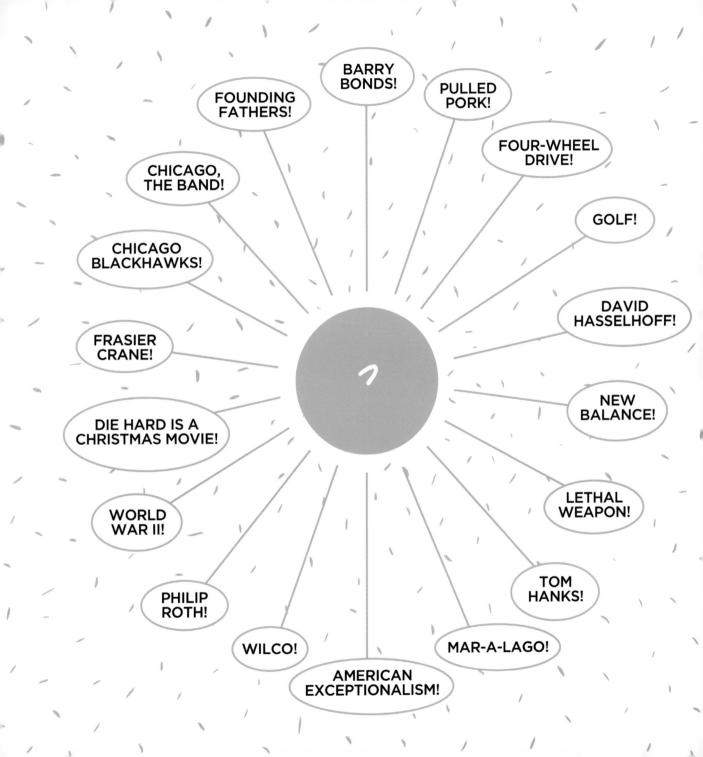

MIDLIFE CRISIS DAD

Perhaps the most easily identifiable of all the dads, the Midlife Crisis Dad is also among the most complex because he exists in a phase that (with any luck) will go as suddenly as it came.

You can spot the Midlife Crisis Dad through extreme and misguided changes in appearance—maybe he starts wearing a puka shell necklace or a leather jacket—or more extreme life choices like divorcing his wife to run off with his colleague Colleen (in a midlife crisis of her own) or, worse, going to surf camp. His car is flashy and impractical (who gets a convertible in the winter?), but he doesn't care. Death is around the corner, baby, and this dad is gonna live it up while he can, hair pieces and all.

FOLLOW DAD ON HIS JOURNEY TO SELF (RE)DISCOVERY

Crashes motorcycle, encounters second brush with death.

Decides to invest in a motorcycle.

Buys sports car instead.

Makes daring hair choice, either buying a toupee, or growing out a ponytail that doesn't quite work with his balding head.

Goes to Costa Rica on a walkabout, really feels like he connected with the ocean/his true self while alone.

Experiences major health scare, recovers.

Last bratty kid goes to college.

Converts basement into a designated "man cave," because he needs some space for himself and his friends, absent from touches of femininity.

Returns home and tells wife that this is the first time in a long time that he's done something just for him.

Celebrates his 45–59 birthday.

Stumbles upon a box of old Jim Croce albums when cleaning out the garage.

Wife asks whom, if not just him, the man cave, motorcycle, and sports car were for? Shushes wife and reiterates how free it felt to travel in solitude.

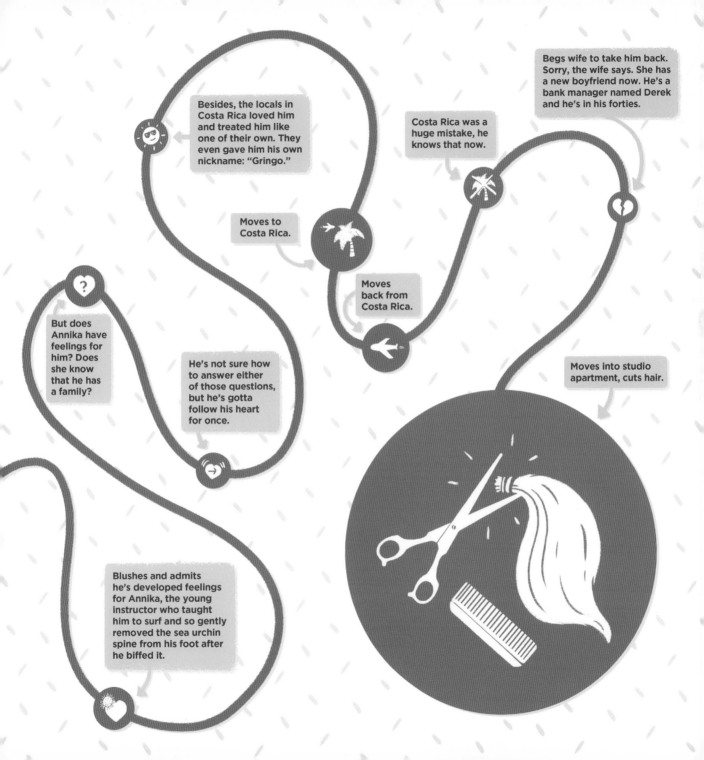

Besides, the locals in Costa Rica loved him and treated him like one of their own. They even gave him his own nickname: "Gringo."

Moves to Costa Rica.

Costa Rica was a huge mistake, he knows that now.

Begs wife to take him back. Sorry, the wife says. She has a new boyfriend now. He's a bank manager named Derek and he's in his forties.

Moves back from Costa Rica.

But does Annika have feelings for him? Does she know that he has a family?

He's not sure how to answer either of those questions, but he's gotta follow his heart for once.

Moves into studio apartment, cuts hair.

Blushes and admits he's developed feelings for Annika, the young instructor who taught him to surf and so gently removed the sea urchin spine from his foot after he biffed it.

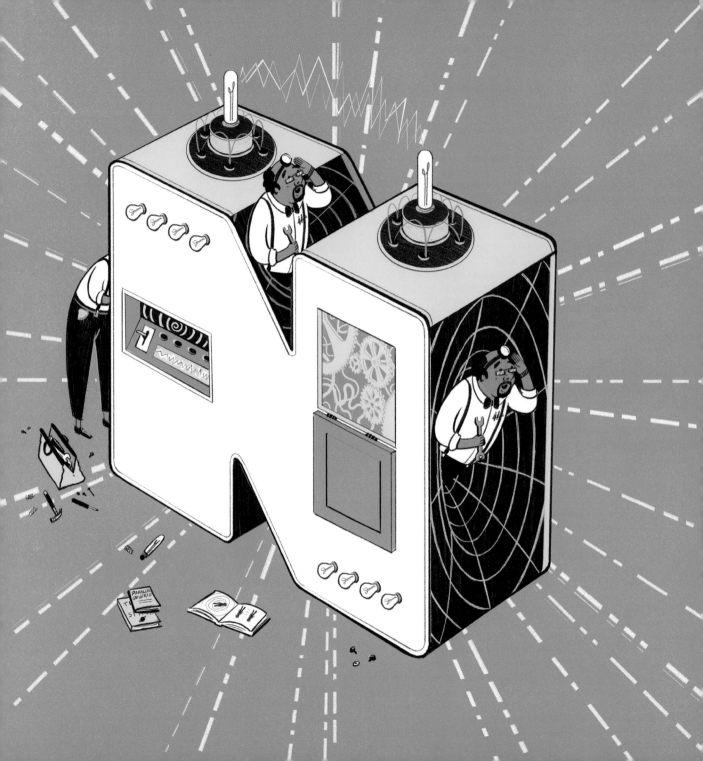

NERD DAD

As endearing as he's enthusiastic, the Nerd Dad just wants the world to love what he loves. Standing in his way, however, are two things: He can sometimes be a know-it-all because he truly does believe that he knows it all when it comes to his chosen passion; and also that the thing he loves—be it astronomy, model trains, or comic books—isn't terribly accessible (or interesting) to the layman.

But, hey, that's okay! The Nerd Dad—probably a nerd since childhood—is used to the outskirts, and celebrates his nerdy otherness in his most well-adjusted form. If you want to make him happy, take him to Comic Con or ask if he wants to watch a few episodes of *Cosmos* (whether he chooses the Carl Sagan or the Neil deGrasse Tyson version depends on the father). If you want to get him angry, intentionally confuse *Star Trek: The Next Generation* and *Star Trek: Enterprise* or tell him that Jar Jar Binks is your favorite part of *Star Wars*.

MERCURY: THE LITERARY NERD DAD. His bookshelf is full of worn and bookmarked leather-bound covers of everything from Chaucer to Melville to Hemingway. He spouts off Shakespeare quotes whenever apt, and often when most annoying. But you wouldn't change him for the world because, as the saying goes, "To thine own self be true." (The Literary Nerd Dad will tell you that this line from *Hamlet* is actually ironic. He's right, but ignore him.)

VENUS: THE TRIVIA NERD DAD. Ever met a dad that seems to know about practically EVERYTHING, be it Sumatran weddings (the bride and groom wear red!), horses (they're measured in "hands," not feet), or architecture (the cornerstone of the White House was laid on October 13, 1792)? He is a trivia nerd, so if you have a trivia night in your future, book him in advance because he'll be in high demand.

JUPITER: THE NOW COOL NERD DAD. In younger days, he was the kid who got shoved into lockers by dumb jocks, but then he went to college, got tall (he was a late bloomer), discovered plaid and square-rimmed glasses, and found a community that valued intelligence and considered it cool. Now he has a great job teaching film studies at the local college, while the kids who bullied him are . . . well, who cares?

EARTH: THE BIOLOGY NERD DAD. He loves his garden and can identify even the most obscure of plants by their taxonomic rank. Go for a hike in the woods and he'll spend hours identifying animal tracks and dissecting owl pellets to proudly show you the tiny bones inside, completely unbothered by handling poop. He loves the ocean and is intrigued rather than terrified of its mysterious depths. Ask him about the weather and you'll get a thirty-minute lecture on meteorology. Litter in front of him and you will break his heart.

MARS: THE SPORTS NERD DAD. If you're looking for him, there's a good chance that he's in front of the TV watching ESPN. To him, seasons are defined not by the weather, but by the sport (i.e., baseball season, football season, hockey season, and basketball season). He cries while watching *Field of Dreams* and, while he might forget your birthday every once in awhile, he can tell you off the top of his head that the Steelers won the 1979 Super Bowl.

a GALAXY of NERD DADS

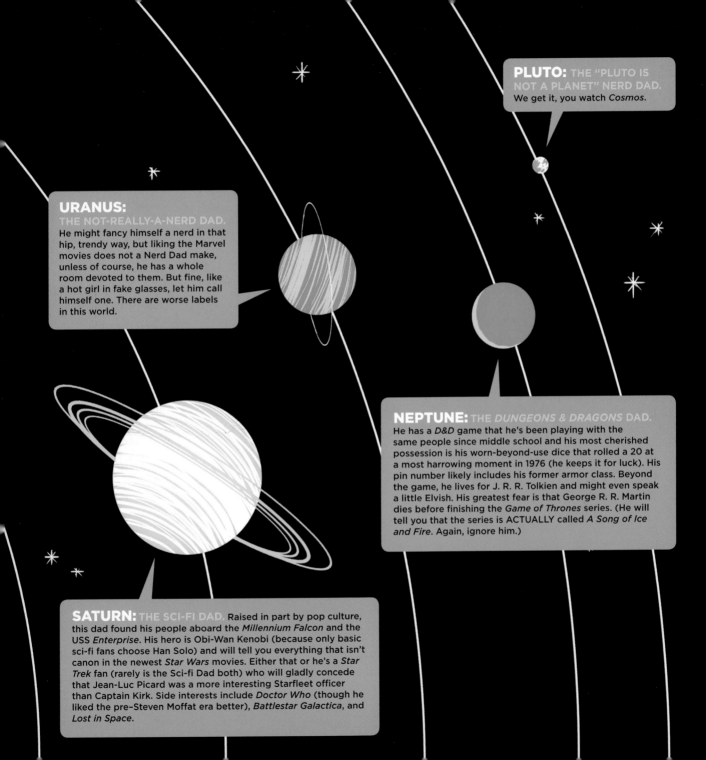

PLUTO: THE "PLUTO IS NOT A PLANET" NERD DAD. We get it, you watch *Cosmos*.

URANUS: THE NOT-REALLY-A-NERD DAD. He might fancy himself a nerd in that hip, trendy way, but liking the Marvel movies does not a Nerd Dad make, unless of course, he has a whole room devoted to them. But fine, like a hot girl in fake glasses, let him call himself one. There are worse labels in this world.

NEPTUNE: THE *DUNGEONS & DRAGONS* DAD. He has a *D&D* game that he's been playing with the same people since middle school and his most cherished possession is his worn-beyond-use dice that rolled a 20 at a most harrowing moment in 1976 (he keeps it for luck). His pin number likely includes his former armor class. Beyond the game, he lives for J. R. R. Tolkien and might even speak a little Elvish. His greatest fear is that George R. R. Martin dies before finishing the *Game of Thrones* series. (He will tell you that the series is ACTUALLY called *A Song of Ice and Fire*. Again, ignore him.)

SATURN: THE SCI-FI DAD. Raised in part by pop culture, this dad found his people aboard the *Millennium Falcon* and the USS *Enterprise*. His hero is Obi-Wan Kenobi (because only basic sci-fi fans choose Han Solo) and will tell you everything that isn't canon in the newest *Star Wars* movies. Either that or he's a *Star Trek* fan (rarely is the Sci-fi Dad both) who will gladly concede that Jean-Luc Picard was a more interesting Starfleet officer than Captain Kirk. Side interests include *Doctor Who* (though he liked the pre–Steven Moffat era better), *Battlestar Galactica*, and *Lost in Space*.

OVERPROTECTIVE DAD

Similar to the Killjoy Dad, the Overprotective Dad sees danger everywhere: the passing of unfamiliar vehicles, sleepovers at a friend's house, and the darkest recesses of their child's prom date. Their job as they see it is to protect you through everything, even after you've reached the point where you can, should, and *want* to protect yourself. Not that it bothers you! The Overprotective Dad typically has nothing but good (though often misguided) intentions and just wants to know that his babies are safe.

The downsides of this particular father variation is that he tends to be controlling and you, his child, will miss out on certain, more reckless experiences growing up. (Maybe those keggers he wouldn't let you go to would have been formative, who knows!) The upside, however, is that this is a father who loves you enough to *not* let you do all the dumb stuff that your child or teen brain is telling you to do.

DAD LIBS!
A First Date Interview

Come on in and take a seat, young _____ [noun] , I'd like to talk to the

_____ [noun] that's about to take my teenage _____ [noun] to _____ [place or event] .

Wow, that's quite a handshake you have there, what are you trying

to do? _____ [verb] my hand off? Just kidding, I can _____ [verb] it. In

fact, I served time in the _____ [name of institution] , so you know I'm _____ [adjective] .

Not that you should let that scare you, or maybe you should!

Would you like a(n) _____ [alcoholic beverage] ? Yes, that was a

test. I wanted to see if you'd _____ [verb] it, which would be very

irresponsible, especially when you're about to _____ [verb] away with

my darling _____ [noun] . You know that _____ [same noun] is precious to

me, right? So precious that I would _____ [verb] for them. Seriously,

if they got _____ [verb, past tense] or _____ [verb, past tense] I'd never be able to

forgive myself, but mostly I wouldn't be able to _____ [verb] you ever

again. That's right, _____ [noun] . I would _____ [verb] you limb from

limb with my _____ [adjective] hands if any harm comes to my dear one.

Now, now, I know you're a(n) _____ [adverb] young _____ [noun] with a

good reputation for _____ [verb] -ing, but you need to understand. It's

not everyday, that I—a _____ [noun] —send my baby into the world. So

be sure and _____ [verb] slowly and carefully, and to have them home

by _____ [time of day] . If not, you will be deeply, deeply _____ [adjective] .

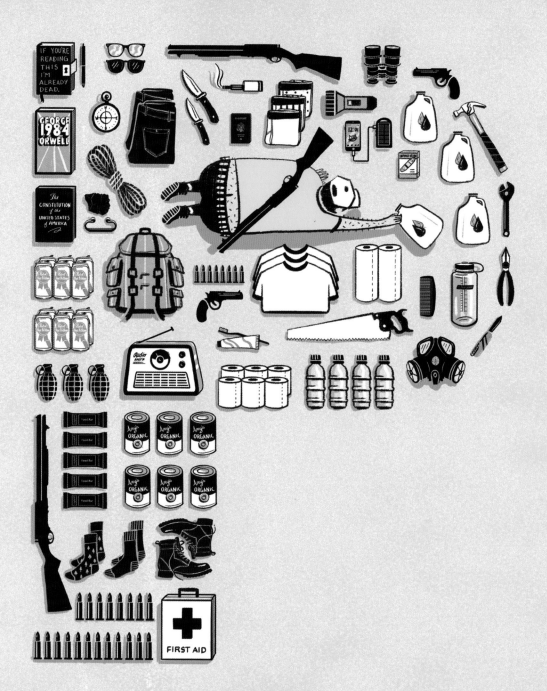

PREPPER DAD

No matter what we write about the Prepper Dad, he—after spending his entire day reading survival guides on Reddit—will likely dismiss it as a conspiracy theory created by Big Pharma, the Illuminati, or the Environmental Protection Agency. But we'll try to do it anyway.

Using his free time to build out his bomb shelter, the Prepper Dad is getting ready for the end of the world, which could either happen at the hand of God, the forthcoming resource wars, the next natural disaster, or because Second Amendment critics are coming to take his guns away. This father can be a little scary, but is great if and when you need to borrow some canned corn (he has literally hundreds), or turn your urine into potable water.

Stumble upon the woodsier Prepper Dad and he might teach you how to build a fire using only your own hair or turn a leather belt into a food source. Run into the more basement-dwelling Prepper Dad and you might only get a long-winded rant against single-patient health care and overreaching government. While these options might sound exhausting to you, we'll see whose reinforced concrete door you're knocking on come the apocalypse.

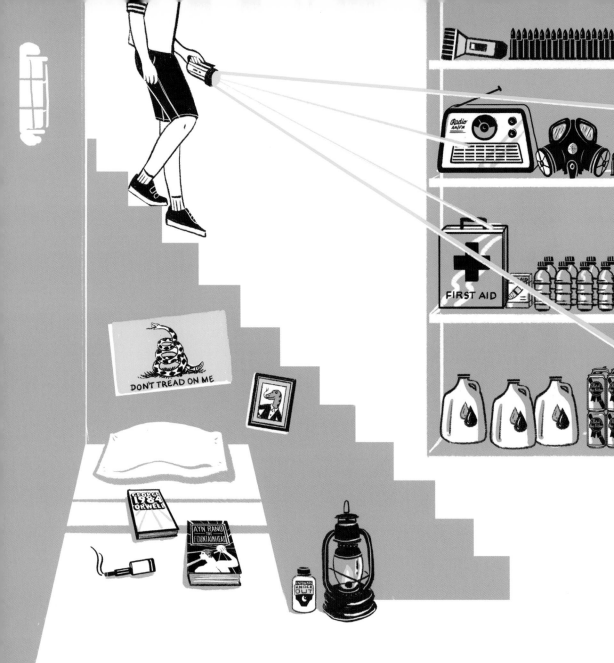

WHAT'S in DAD'S BOMB SHELTER?

Find the gas mask, the portrait of a lizard person, the Ayn Rand book, the can of Spam, gold bullion, and Alex Jones's Infowars supplements.

QUALITY DAD

You ever meet that person who just thinks their dad is the bee's knees? Or maybe *you* are that person. If that's the case, congratulations! You have a Quality Dad—the kind of guy who's as excited to put on a tiara and play tea party as he is to coach his kid's soccer team. Patient and kind, he's where you turn in times of turmoil and somehow he always knows the right thing to say. It's not that you've never disagreed—it's that he shows up for you even when he thinks you're wrong and won't give you too hard of a time when he turns out to be right.

The Quality Dad's skill set includes, but is not limited to: playing catch, hair braiding, comfortable silences, heart-to-heart chats, teaching you how to drive, reminding you to respect your mother, doing his share of household chores, pep talks, jump-starting your car, tight hugs, and tough love.

DAD HACKS

THEY'RE HACKS for DADS!

If you can't duck it, *F*** IT*.

Turn chores like washing the car or picking up toys into a game so that kids don't hate doing it!

Paint a target in the toilet for potty training and a fun activity for you, as well.

Learn how to brush long hair and do a basic braid.

 Untangle doll (not human) hair with dish soap and conditioner or fabric softener.

 Toothpaste can clean permanent marker off of furniture!

 Use a lint roller or tape to clean up craft areas.

 You can lower the volume on annoying toys by putting tape over the speakers.

 Always carry a snack (good for dads and non-dads alike).

 Trick your kids into enjoying your favorite cartoons.

 Don't have a mixer to make cookies for your kid's bake sale? Use an electric drill instead!*

*One of our dads really does this.

ROCK DAD

Careful that you don't cut yourself because this is a dad . . . *with edge*. Either a musician or a man obsessed with musicians, the Rock Dad never forgets that MUSIC IS LIFE. He takes up most of his habitat with his encyclopedic record collection and a variety of guitars that—though he may never admit it—are mainly decorative. He will vary with regards to his chosen genre: Some dads like yacht rock; others like roots rock or classic rock or—for the real bad boys—punk rock.

With a wardrobe consisting solely of work wear, old jeans, and band T-shirts, the Rock Dad likely has some wild (if not *sliiiiightly* embellished) stories, like his time at Altamont (he was driving on the freeway) or Woodstock (1994). No matter what, the guy has heart—a heart that will always belong to you (ideally) and rock and roll (absolutely).

WAYS *into* ROCK DAD'S HEART

ALTERNATIVE ROCK DAD

If you want an Alternative Rock Dad to like you: **Pixies**

If you want an Alternative Rock Dad to love you: **Sonic Youth**

Band/musician he won't admit to liking, but secretly loves: **Foo Fighters**

BLUES-ROCK DAD

If you want a Blues-Rock Dad to like you: **B.B. King**

If you want Blues-Rock Dad to love you: **Muddy Waters**

Band/musician he won't admit to liking, but secretly loves: **Jack White**

GLAM ROCK

If you want a Glam Rock Dad to like you: **David Bowie**

If you want a Glam Rock Dad to love you: **T. Rex**

Band/musician he won't admit to liking, but secretly loves: **Queen**

HAIR METAL

If you want a Hair Metal Dad to like you: **Def Leppard**

If you want a Hair Metal Dad to love you: **Skid Row**

Band/musician he won't admit to liking, but secretly loves: **Bon Jovi**

HARD ROCK

If you want a Hard Rock Dad to like you: **Led Zepplin**

If you want a Hard Rock Dad to love you: **Black Sabbath**

Band/musician he won't admit to liking, but secretly loves: **Tool**

METAL

If you want a Metal Dad to like you: **Metallica**

If you want a Metal Dad to love you: **Pantera**

Band/musician he won't admit to liking, but secretly loves: **Korn**

JAM BAND

If you want a Jam Band Dad to like you: **Dead & Company (Grateful Dead without Jerry Garcia)**

If you want a Jam Band Dad to love you: **Grateful Dead (with Jerry Garcia)**

Band/musician he won't admit to liking, but secretly loves: **Dave Matthews Band**

PSYCHEDELIC ROCK

If you want a Psychedelic Rock Dad to like you: **Jimi Hendrix**

If you want a Psychedelic Rock Dad to love you: **Pink Floyd**

Band/musician he won't admit to liking, but secretly loves: **The Doors**

CLASSIC ROCK AND ROLL

If you want a Classic Rock and Roll Dad to like you: **Elvis**

If you want a Classic Rock and Roll Dad to love you: **Chuck Berry**

Band/musician he won't admit to liking, but secretly loves: **Bill Haley & His Comets**

ROOTS ROCK

If you want a Roots Rock Dad to like you: **Crosby, Stills, Nash & Young**

If you want a Roots Rock Dad to love you: **Bonnie Raitt**

Band/musician he won't admit to liking, but secretly loves:
The Avett Brothers

SINGER/SONGWRITER

If you want a Singer/Songwriter Dad to like you: **Bob Dylan**

If you want a Singer/Songwriter Dad to love you: **Joni Mitchell**

Band/musician he won't admit to liking, but secretly loves:
Ed Sheeran

PUNK ROCK

If you want a Punk Rock Dad to like you: **The Clash**

If you want a Punk Rock Dad to love you: **Hüsker Dü**

Band/musician he won't admit to liking, but secretly loves:
The Replacements

STEP DAD

As the joke goes, "You can pick your friends, you can pick your nose, but you can't pick your parents." That goes double for *step* parents, particularly a Stepdad—the kind of guy who steps into a fractured family whether he's welcome or not.

But go easy on the Stepdad! While the idea of your parents' dating is likely gag-worthy, this is scary for him, too! He's just a guy, after all, which means that he will likely make some mistakes, whether it's making himself *too* comfortable in your home or never settling in quite right.

Only time will tell if you'll grow to love him (or, alternately, if you can successfully *Parent Trap* your parents back together), but for now all you need to know is that he's NOT YOUR REAL DAD, something you're sure to tell him often.

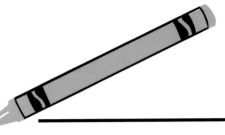

```
B K K C I D H K W T
V D W E L U B E L R
J I G A I Q G V L E
J E R R Y T L I L B
S R F K H B H N I O
Y I C F K M O V B R
M I N C E R B B N Q
D E U N F V X I E T
B H A H E F E T K V
C O Q Z S D G T S O
A T J T T O C S S M
G A R Y C C R N P M
T E D B P I J J C A
D R A H C I R S M R
U T H K D D O T N K
```

- ☑ BILL
- ☐ BOB
- ☐ CHUCK
- ☐ DENNIS
- ☐ DICK (official) ⊢ either as a stand-alone name or nickname for Richard (see below)
- ☐ DICK (unofficial) ⊢ muttered sotto voce, so your Stepdad can't hear
- ☐ ED
- ☐ GARY
- ☐ JEFF ⊢ (he prefers Jeffery, but you call him "Jeff" to annoy him)
- ☐ JERRY
- ☐ KEITH
- ☐ KEN
- ☐ KEVIN
- ☐ LARRY
- ☐ MARK
- ☐ RICHARD
- ☐ RICK
- ☐ ROBERT
- ☐ RON
- ☐ SCOTT
- ☐ STEVE
- ☐ TED
- ☐ TODD

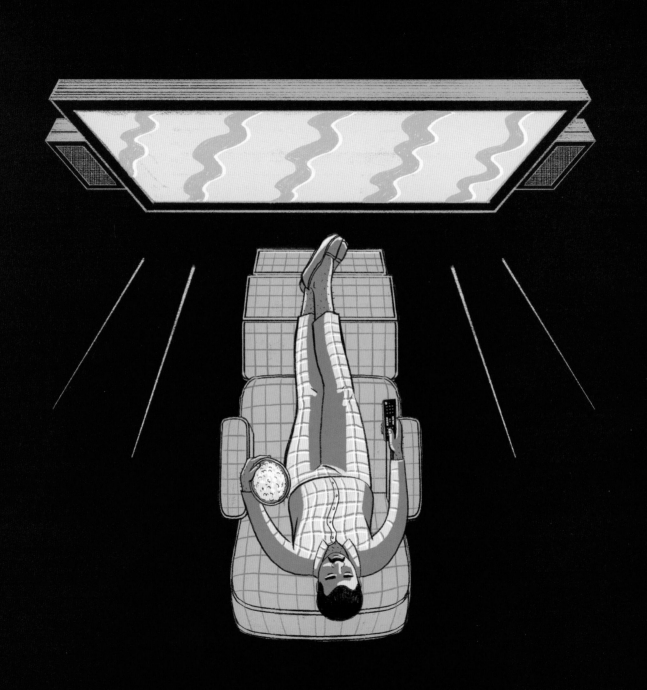

TV DAD

Here's a riddle for you: What's all across the world, but always in one place? It's the TV Dad! Sure, he may exist in every city, town, country, or hamlet, but you can always find him in his favorite spot in front of the television, eyes glazed over as he watches his favorite shows.

His tastes will vary—for some dads, it's sports, others, the news, and then there are those who watch literally everything, from prestige dramas (he'd love to tell you his fan theories on *Game of Thrones*) to your most basic of sitcoms (QUIET, a rerun of *King of Queens* is on). Whatever he loves to watch, it is best not to fight him on it. This is where he feels safest and the most at home. We should all be so lucky to have a place like that.

Now hand dad the remote control.

WARD CLEAVER
Leave It to Beaver

MIKE BRADY
The Brady Bunch

TV DADS

JASON SEAVER
Growing Pains

CARL WINSLOW
Family Matters

RUPERT GILES
Buffy the Vampire Slayer

TONY SOPRANO
The Sopranos

RANDY MARSH
South Park

GEORGE JEFFERSON
The Jeffersons

CHARLES INGALLS
Little House on the Prairie

CLIFF HUXTABLE
The Cosby Show

PHILIP BANKS
Fresh Prince of Bel-Air

DANNY TANNER
Full House

HOMER SIMPSON
The Simpsons

DONALD DRAPER
Mad Men

WALTER WHITE
Breaking Bad

BOB BELCHER
Bob's Burgers

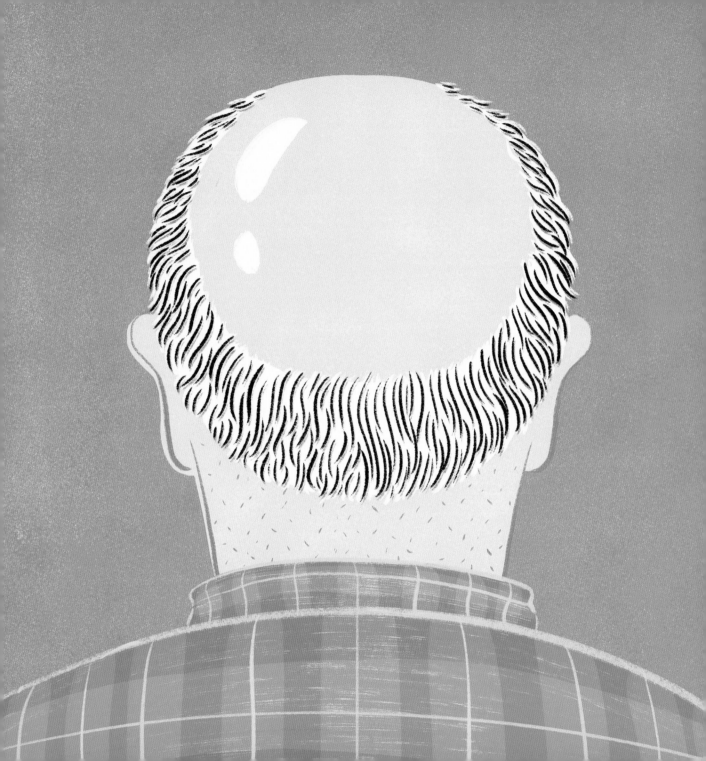

UNAVAILABLE DAD

Look, not everyone can be emotionally fluent or present in the moment. If you have an Unavailable Dad, you likely already knew that and are hopefully well on your way to healing from the hurt caused by his literal or figurative abandonment.

Maybe your dad went out for cigarettes and never came back. Or maybe he's sitting across from you as you read this book, finding new and hurtful ways to distance himself from you. Either way . . . he sucks. You rule. He doesn't know what he's missing.

HOW WILL YOU GET DAD'S ATTENTION?

DAD IS TAKING HIS POST WORK NAP? DO YOU:
- A. Quietly work on your homework (getting it done means more time with dad when he's awake!) as not to wake and annoy him?
- B. Watch TV on a low volume until he gets up?
- C. Go to a friend's house because home is boring?
- D. Be as loud as possible on purpose?

WHICH OF DAD'S HOBBIES DO YOU WANT TO BE A PART OF?
- A. Anything! What dad loves, you love!
- B. Bowling. At least it will be fun for you, too.
- C. You really do not care about Dad's hobbies.
- D. Anything you can disrupt and ruin for him!

IT'S YOUR BIRTHDAY. HOW DOES DAD SIGN YOUR CARD?
- A. "Proud of ya."
- B. "—Dad"
- C. Mom clearly signed it for him
- D. He remembered it was my birthday???

WHEN YOU SEE DAD AFTER A LONG TIME AWAY, HOW DOES HE GREET YOU?
- A. An awkward one-armed hug after you go in for the full thing
- B. A pat on the shoulder
- C. A handshake
- D. A nod

WHAT'S YOUR FAVORITE FAMILY SHOW?
- A. *The Brady Bunch*
- B. *The Simpsons*
- C. *Married...with Children*
- D. *The Jerry Springer Show*

YOU ACCIDENTALLY BREAK DAD'S MOST CHERISHED ITEM. DO YOU:

A. Panic, bury the pieces and hope he never notices?
B. Own up to it and face the consequences?
C. Shove it in a drawer, because whatever, who cares?
D. Break more items? At least when he's yelling at you, he's also noticing you!

WHO IS DAD'S BEST FRIEND?

A. You, you hope!
B. A tie between his friend Bill and your mother
C. Who knows? Some guys?
D. The town law enforcement, because you're a punk that keeps getting arrested and they've struck up a bond.

WHAT'S YOUR MOST CHERISHED FAMILY MEMORY?

A. Any time the whole family is together
B. When your parents took you to Disneyland
C. Nothing stands out
D. When you egged your dad's car and he was so mad, hahaha!

IT'S REPORT CARD TIME! TALLY UP YOUR ANSWERS TO SEE IF YOU GOT:

A. Mostly As
B. Mostly Bs
C. Mostly Cs
D. Mostly Ds

MOSTLY As
Oh, my sweet soul. You're trying to get dad's attention by overachieving. It's a noble effort that will take you far in life, but only to disappointing places with your father. On the bright side, he might apologize for his neglect on his deathbed!

MOSTLY Bs
Look, you're just trying to make it to adulthood as adjusted as possible. You know that this could be a lost cause, but that's what therapy is for.

MOSTLY Cs
You have taught yourself not to care one bit (or at least ACT like you don't care one bit) and are biding your time until you can move out and get your own place.

MOSTLY Ds
You get attention through destruction and acting out! It's certainly an effective methodology, but ultimately self-harming. Rise above your circumstances (meaning your dad's crappy parenting) and get your life together! Happier times await!

VACATION DAD

The Vacation Dad is the rare dad that exists in specific circumstances, but not in perpetuity (unless, of course, he decides at retirement to drive across the country in a RV). Any dad *can* be a Vacation Dad, though some are certainly more prone to it.

A Vacation Dad *loves* organized fun, but is cursed to exist in a state of constant stress and chaos as he attempts to ferry his family from Niagara Falls to Mount Rushmore to Disneyland. Most commonly found shouting at his kids for misbehaving in the car—or misbehaving at the theme park or misbehaving at the museum or Gettysburg or the beach—his face is almost always red (both from anger and sunburn) and his legs encased in cargo shorts.

Will he ever learn from his past mistakes? Just ask the family travel agent, Karen, who's currently booking the next family vacation to Myrtle Beach.

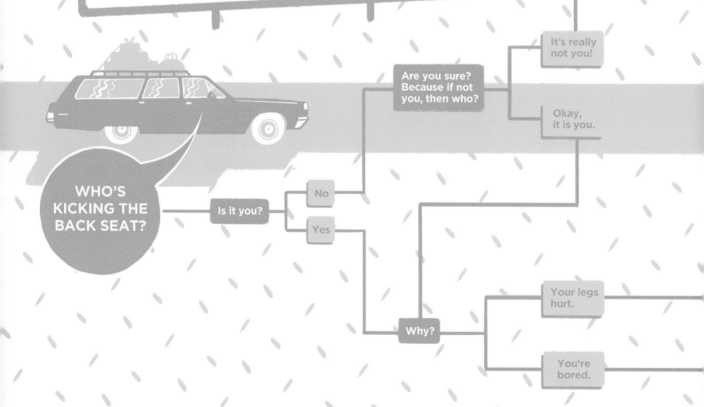

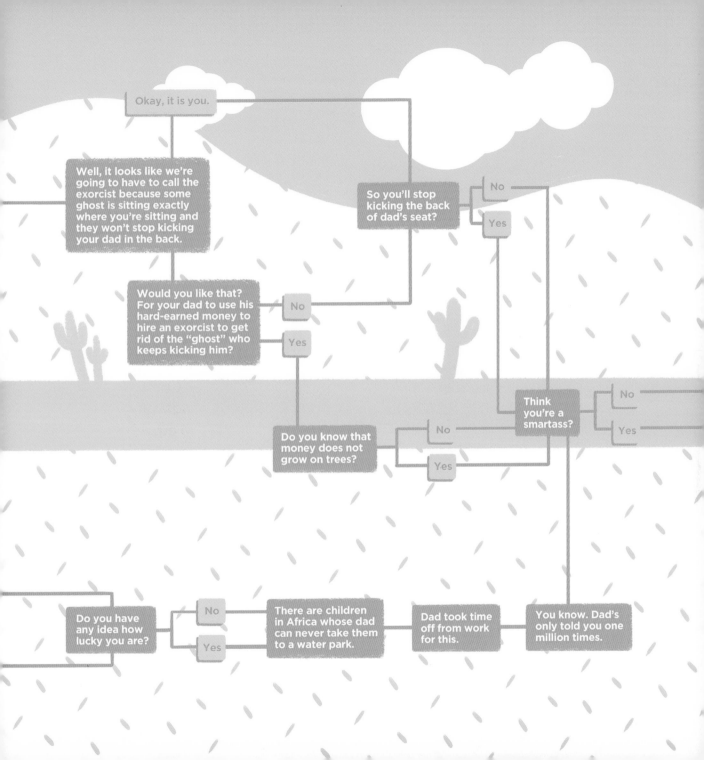

DAD-STINATIONS AROUND the COUNTRY

Space Needle (Seattle, WA)

Mall of America (Bloomington, MN)

Old Faithful (Yellowstone National Park, WY)

Mount Rushmore (Keystone, SD)

Wall Drug (Wall, SD)

Rock & Roll Hall of Fame (Cleveland, OH)

Gettysburg (Gettysburg, PA)

The Liberty Bell (Philadelphia, PA)

Lucasfilm (San Francisco, CA)

Yosemite (Sierra Nevada mountains, CA)

Colonial Williamsburg (Williamsburg, VA)

Four Corners (Utah, Colorado, Arizona, and New Mexico border)

Disneyland (Anaheim, CA)

Graceland (Memphis, TN)

Talladega Superspeedway (Talladega, AL)

The Alamo (San Antonio, TX)

Cape Canaveral (Cape Canaveral, FL)

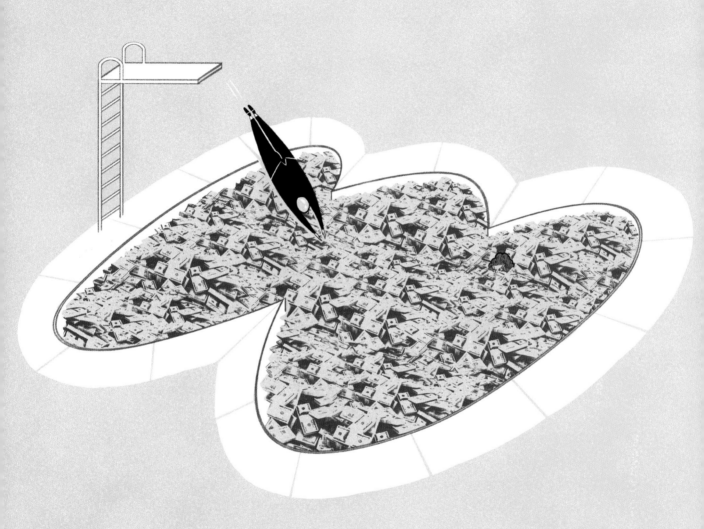

WARBUCKS DAD

Are you a charismatic pupil-less orphan with curly red hair who was plucked out of an orphanage to live with a single rich man and his oddly dedicated and beautiful assistant? Do you sing and dance through hardship, always looking forward to "Tomorrow! Tomorrow! I love ya, tomorrow" because it's "always a day away" and surely there are happier experiences ahead? Then one, you might be Annie and two, you have a Daddy Warbucks, a gruff albeit kindhearted business man, who—lucky you—decides to adopt you.

In less appealing news, it's the middle of the Depression, you've lost your parents, and are a work of fiction. Don't feel too disappointed. After all, "the sun will come out..."

WHAT RAGS-to-RICHES ORPHAN ARE YOU?

WHERE DID YOU GROW UP?
A. An orphanage
B. With your mean relatives
C. With your nice relatives
D. A workhouse

WHAT IS YOUR BEST QUALITY?
A. Your optimism
B. Your special talents
C. Your feisty personality
D. You're always willing to ask for more

WHO IS YOUR STAND-IN PARENTAL FIGURE?
A. An extremely wealthy industrialist
B. Your school headmaster
C. Two elderly siblings you were sent to by mistake
D. A gang of ragamuffins and an their anti-semitic caricature of a leader

WHAT'S YOUR FAVORITE OUTFIT?
A. A kicky red dress
B. Your school uniform
C. Anything you can work the farm in
D. You're just happy to have clothes!

WHO IS YOUR BEST FRIEND?

A. Your dog
B. Your school friends
C. Your crush
D. A streetwise pickpocket

WHAT'S YOUR MOTTO?

A. The sun will come out tomorrow!
B. *Sssssssssss.*
C. It's been my experience that you can nearly always enjoy things if you make up your mind firmly that you will.
D. Where is love?

MOSTLY A'S
You're the princess of positivity, the optimum at optimism—little orphan Annie herself! It might be a hard-knock life, but rarely do you let that get you down. You don't dwell on the past and instead look until…you get it.

MOSTLY B'S
Expect your invite to Hogwarts soon because you're Harry Potter, the boy who lived! The sad news is that life, which has never been easy for you, won't get easier for quite a while, but the GOOD news is that you always get by with a little help from your friends. Plus, you can speak the language of snakes!

MOSTLY C'S
The second Anne on our list, you—Anne of Green Gables—are a true spitfire and while your spunk often gets you into trouble (or leads you to put your foot in your mouth) it's also what makes you impossible NOT to love. Crack open a Prince Edward Island oyster, tip it back, and ENJOY.

MOSTLY D'S
You're Oliver! Whether you're derived from Charles Dickens' novel *Oliver Twist*, the musical *Oliver!*, or the cartoon *Oliver & Company* (in which Oliver is an adorable kitten), your rough beginnings (a workhouse, poor thing!) is no match for your inherent sweetness. Your path to the high life will not be easy, but you'll make plenty of friends along the way.

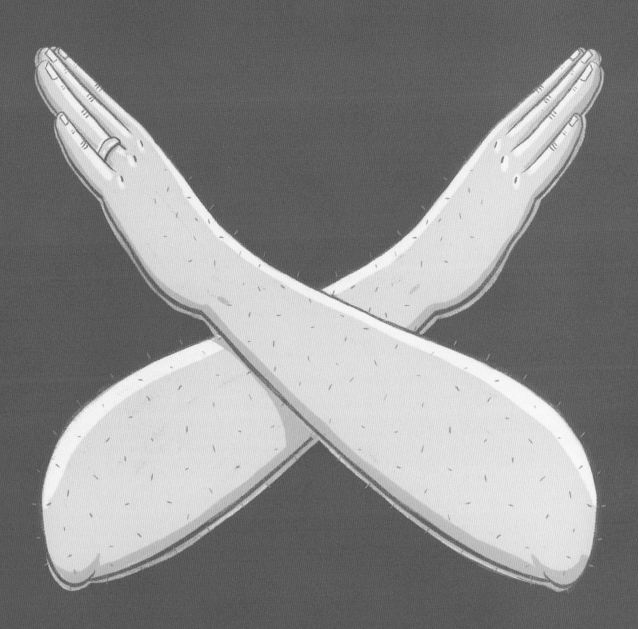

XENOPHOBIC DAD

The Xenophobic Dad scorns progress—often loudly in public places or at family gatherings. Terrified of change and upending the social order, he channels his anxieties into anger against certain groups of people, though the group he zeroes in on the most is anyone's guess, making this the worst guessing game of all time.

If this is your dad, you probably fight constantly in the hopes that one day you will break through to him and open him to the possibility that we might not *need* a wall between the United States and Mexico, or the United States and Canada, for that matter. Maybe he'll one day accept that your same-sex partner is not actually your roommate and, yes, gay marriage should be legal.

Keep going! It's hard work you're doing, but hey, it might just work—though you'll have to sit through a lot of stressful and shout-y Sunday night dinners to get there.

IT'S the HOLIDAYS!

CAN YOU AVOID a FIGHT with DAD?

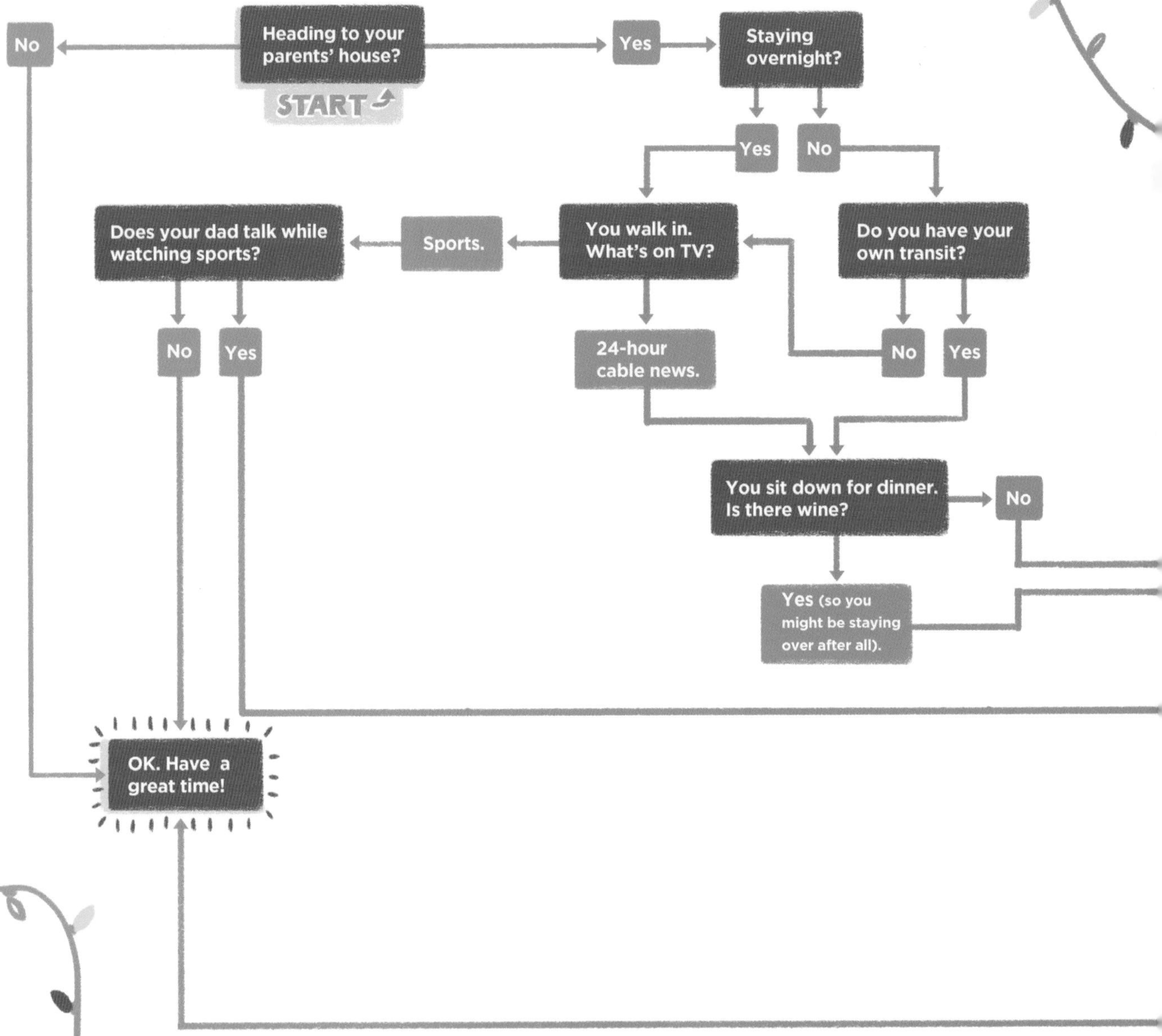

Heading to your parents' house? START ↵

No

Yes → **Staying overnight?**

Yes | No

Yes → **You walk in. What's on TV?**

No → **Do you have your own transit?**

Does your dad talk while watching sports? ← Sports. ← **You walk in. What's on TV?**

No | Yes

24-hour cable news.

No | Yes

You sit down for dinner. Is there wine? → No

Yes (so you might be staying over after all).

OK. Have a great time!

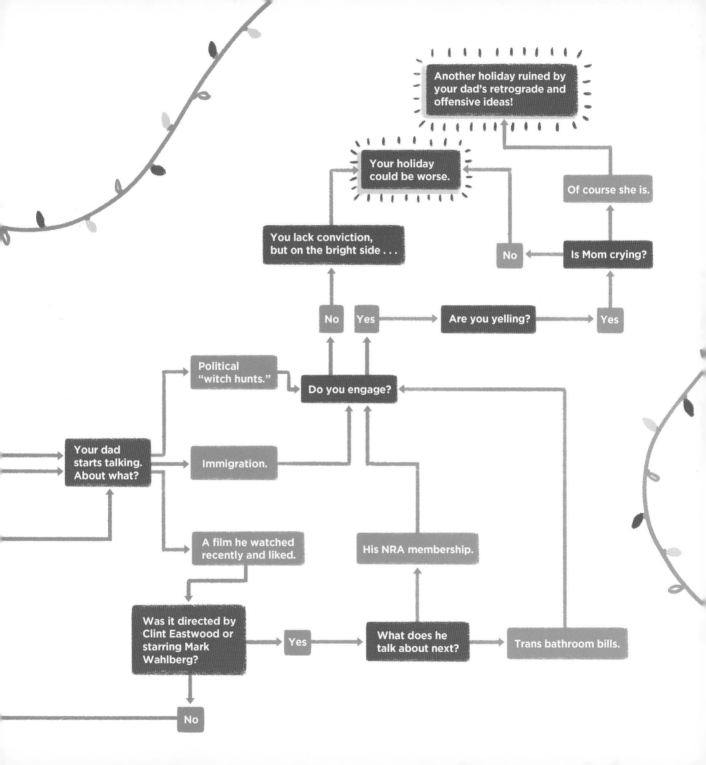

YUPPIE DAD

There's comfort in the cookie-cutter life, as demonstrated by the Yuppie Dad with his luxury SUV and middle-management job (retirement is only a few years away!). He prides himself on his pristine lawn and the basement rec room that he's converted into a "man cave" where he hosts his friends on Super Bowl Sunday, treating them to buffalo wings and cool brews.

While it's easy to mock the Yuppie Dad for his contentment with suburban normalcy, it's just as easy to envy him. We should all be so lucky to find joy tinkering around in a garage, dressing in Dockers, and kicking back at the end of the day in his La-Z-Boy, which by the way, has a mini fridge in the armrest.

Ride on in that riding lawn mower, Yuppie Dad. Ride on.

END

ZADDY

What's a "Zaddy"? Depends who you ask. Most will tell you that a Zaddy is any attractive older man who makes you drool. Others will tell you it's any guy who makes you say, *"Zamn Zaddy."* Regardless, a Zaddy is basically a Sugar Daddy (not included in *this* edition), only this Sugar Daddy is handsome, fun to be around, AND rich.

Popularized by rapper Ty Dolla $ign's song "Zaddy," the term rose in use among young people between 2016 and 2018. Unfortunately, since it is known by *us* (two white women in our thirties), "Zaddy" is no longer cool. Use it at your own peril!

WHO'S YOUR ZADDY?

WHAT IS YOUR FAVORITE TYPE OF MEN'S STYLE?
A. Classic and elegant (i.e., well-tailored suits)
B. Aging hipster (skinny jeans, leather boots, and leather jackets—even in the summer)
C. Hypebeast (extensive sneaker collection, athleisure, and everything Supreme)
D. Classic Dad (can you even call it style when his outfit is purely coincidental instead of a choice?)

WHAT'S YOUR FAVORITE THING TO DO?
A. Drink martinis at a chic cocktail lounge
B. Go to concerts
C. Await the latest sneaker drop (or, more simply, shop)
D. Relax at home

WHAT KIND OF HOUSE DO YOU WANT?
A. A well-appointed penthouse apartment in the city
B. An eccentric bungalow in a cool neighborhood
C. Glass-walled mansion, baby!!!!!!
D. Someplace quiet with a nice yard (and maybe even a woodshed) that you can call your own

FAVORITE MEN'S HAIRCUT?
A. Short, clean edges, and neatly groomed with expensive hair products
B. Dirty, overgrown, and seemingly effortless (when, in fact, it really takes a lot of effort to look this greasy)
C. Bright hair dye in unnatural colors, braids, and unique fades
D. A sensible haircut that he does himself with clippers in the bathroom

PICK A VEHICLE:

A. Jaguar (the car, not the animal) or beamer

B. Something vintage and requiring constant maintenance, but oh-so-cool looking

C. A lamborghini in the flashiest color you can find

D. A reliable four-door that always gets you where you need to go, be it a far-off hiking spot or school drop-off

MOSTLY A'S

Who is he? He's earned his money in hedge funds and loathes the hoodie-laden sloppiness of Silicon Valley millionaires. He is extreme about fitness and his career, and is likely a tad humorless and boring. Not like that really matters when it comes to picking a zaddy. (What does matter: attractiveness, a whole lot of money to support your lifestyle.) **Where can you find him?** Bustling urban environments with thriving business districts. Think NYC, London, Hong Kong. **Who are his celebrity role models?** George Clooney and Idris Elba.

MOSTLY B'S

Who is he? He made his money in the arts (or at least that's what he says to keep you distracted from his massive trust fund) and probably has a pretty big Instagram following even though he thinks Instagram is "dumb." **Where can you find him?** Gentrifying neighborhoods and "working" at various coffee shops in the cool part of town. **Who are his celebrity role models?** He's not "into celebrity," but he loves Jared Leto.

MOSTLY C'S

Who is he? He's a young upstart who's made his money flipping merch and accidentally creating a start-up because he's secretly great at coding. He's fun, a little crazy, and somehow seems to never need to sleep. **Where can you find him?** Energized, fashion-forward cities like Tokyo or Miami. Wherever the other sneaker-heads are at. **Who are his celebrity role models?** Rae Sremmurd, Migos, Tyler the Creator.

MOSTLY D'S

Who is he? Just a normal guy who made his millions after creating his own company, selling it, and now spends his days doing the leisure activities (making furniture, mountain biking, urban—or suburban—farming) he loves the most. **Where can you find him?** Greener, more spacious pastures outside of bustling cities (Beacon, New York, Topanga, California, or the entire state of Vermont, for example). **Who are his celebrity role models?** Mark Ruffalo, Jon Stewart, Barack Obama.